NOAH'S ARK

Contributing Writer
Marlene Targ Brill

Consultant
David M. Howard, Jr., Ph.D.

Illustrations
Thomas Gianni

Publications International, Ltd.

One day, many years after God had created Adam and Eve, He looked closely at all the people on earth. There were many more people now. They had forgotten about God and His ways. He could see only evil in their hearts. God decided to start all over again.

God had one faithful servant named Noah. He wanted to save Noah and his family. So God said to Noah, "I am going to put an end to all things as they are now."

God told Noah about His plan and what He wanted Noah to do. "Build yourself an ark, a large boat of wood. I will cause a great rain to flood the earth. But you and your family will be safe."

Noah did as God commanded. He built the ark with help from his three sons, Shem, Ham, and Japheth. Noah's neighbors probably thought he was foolish. Why would anyone build a ship in the middle of dry land?

ጉ ቶ

Then, God told Noah to bring two of each living thing to the ark. There were big and small animals, strong and weak animals, insects and birds of all kinds. Every type of animal you can imagine was going to be on the ark! Noah and his family were going to take care of all these animals.

Once all the animals were together, God told Noah to take clothing and food for the journey. Noah did all that God ordered.

Later, God spoke to Noah again. He said, "Go into the ark now, you and all who are with you. In seven days I will send rain on the earth. The rain will last forty days and forty nights. Water will wash away everything from the ground."

Noah followed God's instructions. He loaded all the food and animals into the ark. Then he and his family entered the ark.

On the seventh day, God shut the ark. The rain began to fall.

At first, drops of rain fell here and there. But it was not long before great waves of water covered the ground. The water began to get higher and higher. The floodwater was so strong it lifted the ark above the earth. People and animals ran for high places. But there seemed to be water everywhere! Soon water covered every tree and every mountaintop.

Only Noah and those who were with him in the ark had a safe place to stay.

All that could be seen for miles and miles was water and cloudy skies. But inside the ark, Noah, his family, and the animals were safe and warm.

After forty days, God made the rain stop. A bright sun came out and started to dry up all the floodwater.

Little by little, the water went down. Before too long, the mountaintops could be seen peeking through the water. God caused the ark to rest on top of a mountain called Ararat.

One day, Noah opened the ark window and sent out a raven. The raven found no place to land. One week later, Noah sent out a dove. The dove returned to the ark because there was still no place to land.

After another week, Noah sent the dove out again and it came back with a small branch from an olive tree. When Noah sent the dove out once more, it did not return. The bird had found a place to rest. Now Noah knew that all of the floodwater had dried up.

ༀༀ

Noah removed the door from the ark. After such a long time with nothing but water everywhere, Noah could finally see land! There were mountains and plains, hills and valleys. Even the rivers and lakes were all normal again!

God spoke to Noah: "Now leave the ark with your family. Bring out all the animals you cared for. Let them live on earth and start families."

So Noah and everyone on the ark did as God said.

They were all happy to step onto dry land again. They built an altar and prayed, thanking God for keeping them safe.

God heard Noah's prayers and made a promise in His heart: "I will never again destroy the ground because of evil in the human heart."

God set a beautiful rainbow in the sky. "Rainbows will remind you and all future people of my promise," He told Noah. "Whenever a rainbow appears in the clouds, remember my promise."

ታቱ